SCHOLASTIC

First Graphic Organizers
Writing

30 Reproducible Graphic Organizers That Build Essential Early Writing Skills

by Rhonda Graff

NEW YORK • TORONTO • LONDON • AUCKLAND • SYDNEY
MEXICO CITY • NEW DELHI • HONG KONG • BUENOS AIRES

Teaching *Resources*

To Stephen M. Smith—with love and gratitude

Thank you to Gina Shaw, Liza Charlesworth, Jason Robinson, Craig and Daniel, and my parents Stan and Joan

—R.G.

Scholastic Inc. grants teachers permission to photocopy the designated reproducible pages for classroom use. No other part of the publication may be reproduced in whole or in part, or stored in a retrieval system, or transmitted in any way or by any means, electronic, mechanical, photocopying, recording, or otherwise, without written permission of the publisher. For information, write to Scholastic Inc., 524 Broadway, New York, NY 10012.

Cover and design by Jason Robinson

ISBN-13: 978-0-545-15047-7 / ISBN-10: 0-545-15047-7

1 2 3 4 5 6 7 8 9 10   40   09

Contents

Introduction

USING THIS BOOK

Welcome to *First Graphic Organizers: Writing!* The 30 graphic organizers in this book are designed to provide age-perfect scaffolding to help young learners soar as new writers. These classroom-tested organizers are not cookie-cutter forms to fill in or writing exercises to be completed as a class. Rather, they are helpful tools to guide children in the planning, editing, and polishing of their work. Children will compose their rough drafts on separate sheets of paper, using the organizers to support them in the various stages of writing.

The focus of the activities is to encourage children to share their thoughts and ideas, first through storytelling, and then slowly progressing to writing. These organizers will help children get started, plan, and improve their writing—and ultimately, feel more comfortable with the act of writing. The goal is to have children understand the writing process well enough to use these organizers as needed; to change them, if necessary; to develop their own as they gain more experience; and finally to feel more confident as writers. Remember, this takes time, practice, and encouragement. Children will move through the process at their own speed.

Encourage children to share their ideas orally first, then move to free writing. Have them share their ideas and explore the many possibilities of expression. Some children may draw while others may begin to incorporate letters or words or both. Children should be introduced to the importance of correct spelling, sentence formation, punctuation, and capitalization even if they are not yet fully accountable for these in the early phases of writing. Slowly introduce students to the activities, beginning with the brainstorming and sentence writing organizers, and eventually, moving into paragraph and essay writing. When students feel confident as writers, there are no limits!

IMPORTANCE OF SHARING WRITING

It is important to share well-written literature with your students. Being exposed to talented authors provides models for children to emulate. Be sure to comment on interesting use of language, style, and content. Model questioning techniques and share with children things you wonder about as you read. Provide many types of writing, so children can be exposed to a variety of genres. As they progress, children can begin to apply skills and techniques to their own writing. Also, be sure to share their work, validating their successes and accomplishments as authors.

IN EACH UNIT

For each of the 30 organizers, you'll find:

background information about the skill the organizer targets

an indication of whether the organizer should be used for pre-writing, sentence writing, paragraph writing, revising, or as a conference helper

a brief description of the organizer's benefits

ready-to-reproduce pages

an example of a completed organizer

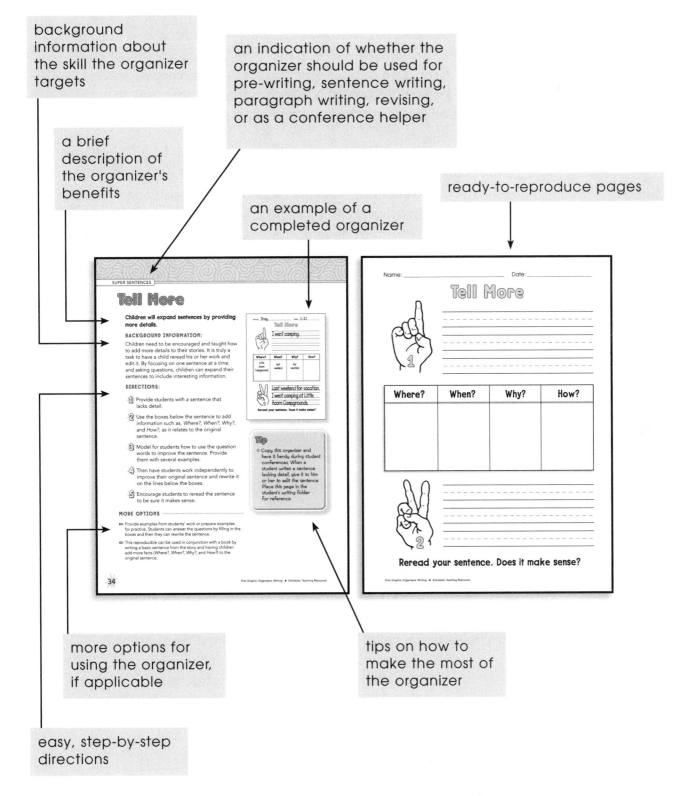

more options for using the organizer, if applicable

tips on how to make the most of the organizer

easy, step-by-step directions

About the Organizers

The organizers are divided into five sections. Although they are presented in a specific order, you should choose and use the organizers as needed for your students, based on their varying abilities. And feel free to use the organizer as it works best for you and your students, since there is no correct or incorrect way to work with it. It is also important for children to know they, too, can offer input as to how the reproducible will best suit their needs. Tell them it's fine to change the organizer or to create their own.

Be sure to model each organizer. Some can be introduced as a whole, while others will require you to model individual sections. Take as much time as needed to model, as a clear understanding of the activity will directly impact the success children have using organizers to aid them in their writing development. Once the activities are modeled and children understand how to use them, the organizers should help students in planning the pieces they are writing. Remember, these organizers are helpers, not end products. And, of course, always encourage students to share their work; there's no better way to learn.

PRE-WRITING

Young children, as well as experienced writers, often have difficulty getting started in their writing. The organizers in this section encourage children to verbally share their stories through pictures and/or using words before they actually write anything down. Drawing, brainstorming, and clustering are used to help children generate ideas and begin writing.

SUPER SENTENCES

The foundation to a good paragraph is a good sentence. Although children can express their ideas without fully understanding what makes a good sentence, sentence structure should be taught to help children make their writing stronger. Children need practice writing well-developed sentences and working with the organizers in this section helps teach children how to write interesting sentences.

Remember, not all children will be ready for formal writing instruction at the same time, regardless of its importance. If children need to share orally, draw, label, or create brainstorming lists for a longer period of time than their peers, let them progress at their own pace. Always look for ways to encourage their steps forward from their current ability levels.

PARAGRAPHS

Young children often don't even know how to "navigate" their paper, let alone how to develop a topic sentence, details, and a concluding sentence. This section introduces indenting and margins and guides children through the planning of a well-developed paragraph.

Once children have practiced writing sentences, they should be able to join their sentences into meaningful, focused paragraphs. Although young children should be given freedom to experiment with their voice and topics, they more than likely need instruction on how to write a paragraph. This section provides some basics as children move into paragraph writing.

REVISING

Revising is one of the most challenging parts of the writing process. Once something is written, most of us are happy it is done. Why should children feel any differently? Although rewarding, rereading and rewriting are not favorite pastimes. Children need to be taught how to reread and how to find words, sentences, and paragraphs that can be improved. The organizers in this section help teach children how to change, add to, delete, and reread in order to enhance their work.

CONFERENCE HELPERS

This section provides conference helpers to be used during writing conferences. In addition to the Conference Log for monitoring each child's progress, there are several half-page and full-page organizers to pinpoint different areas of concern that may arise as children begin writing.

During conferences or Writing Block, have these reproducibles at your fingertips as you observe your students. Consider setting up either a binder with pockets labeled "word space," "margins," "punctuation," etc., or a file folder box, drawer, or trays with the same sections or allocations. That way, you will have reproducibles on hand to assist with some common writing difficulties young children experience. Then, after assisting the student, the handout can be stored in his or her folder for future reference.

Meeting the Language Arts Standards

The graphic organizers in this book are designed to support you in meeting the following standards outlined by the Mid-continent Regional Educational Laboratory (McREL), an organization that collects and synthesizes national and state K-12 curriculum standards.

Writing: Grades 1-3

Uses the general skills and strategies of the writing process

✳ Pre-writing: Uses pre-writing strategies to plan written work (e.g., discusses ideas with peers; draws pictures to generate ideas; writes key thoughts and questions; rehearses ideas; records reactions and observations; uses graphic organizers, story maps, and webs; groups related ideas; takes notes; brainstorms ideas; organizes information according to type and purpose of writing)

✳ Drafting and Revising: Uses strategies to draft and revise written work (e.g., rereads; rearranges words, sentences, and paragraphs to improve or clarify meaning; varies sentence type; adds descriptive words and details; deletes extraneous information; incorporates suggestions from peers and teachers; sharpens the focus)

✳ Evaluates own and others' writing (e.g., asks questions and makes comments about writing; helps classmates apply grammatical and mechanical conventions)

✳ Uses strategies to organize written work (e.g., includes a beginning, middle, and ending)

✳ Uses writing and other methods (e.g., using letters or phonetically spelled words; telling; dictating; making lists) to describe familiar persons, places, objects, or experiences

Uses grammatical and mechanical conventions in written compositions

✷ Uses conventions of print in writing (e.g., forms letters in print, uses upper- and lowercase letters of the alphabet, spaces words and sentences, writes from left-to-right and top-to-bottom, includes margins)

✷ Uses complete sentences in written compositions

✷ Uses conventions of capitalization in written compositions (e.g., first and last names, first word of a sentence)

✷ Uses conventions of punctuation in written compositions (e.g., uses periods after declarative sentences, uses question marks after interrogative sentences)

Uses the stylistic and rhetorical aspects of writing

✷ Uses descriptive words to convey basic ideas

✷ Uses declarative and interrogative sentences in written compositions

Listen Up!

Working as partners, children will verbally share a story and act as storytellers and listeners/recorders.

BACKGROUND INFORMATION:

In the early stages of writing, many children are not ready to actually write. However, they do have many ideas to share. Model this organizer with the class or a small group. Be sure to model both the storyteller role and the listener/recorder role. Modeling is crucial, as children will learn to share great stories and to listen carefully so they can retell and comment on a story. With practice, children will share more elaborate tales, and the listeners/recorders will provide more beneficial feedback.

DIRECTIONS:

1 Group students into pairs. Designate one student as the storyteller and the other student as the listener. If the storyteller wants to take a few minutes to draw or write some ideas in the top box, he or she can. If not, that's fine, too.

2 Have the storyteller tell a story to his or her partner. (You may need to put a time limit on this if stories are running too long.)

3 Encourage the listener to use the bottom box to draw pictures or to write words to help recall information. The listener can also ask questions about the story.

4 When the first child is finished telling the story, have the second child "retell" the story to the storyteller.

5 Have the storyteller and the listener switch places.

Tips

✳ Copy this organizer and place it in students' writing folders for use if children are having difficulty generating ideas. When a student has trouble, this reproducible will serve as a reminder of the value of storytelling and verbally sharing ideas as a brainstorming tool.

✳ Students may wish to keep copies of previously completed Listen Up! reproducibles to use as springboards for future ideas if they get writer's block.

Listen Up!

Storyteller

Listener

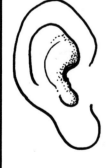

Let's Get Started

Using visualization and question prompts to get started, children will brainstorm a topic, an event, or a memory.

BACKGROUND INFORMATION:

As with all organizers, model the process of brainstorming. Show children how to choose a topic and then elaborate on it using visualization and question prompts. Be sure to describe what you see when you model visualization. Being dramatic about your visualization often helps children create vivid pictures in their own minds during their visualizations. Be sure to review each box on the reproducible. With young children, this will take time. Model often so when children try, they begin with confidence. Over time, children may be able to do some of this planning mentally. It will become more automatic as they become more confident and experienced. Children can draw pictures and/or write words in the boxes to share their ideas and thoughts.

DIRECTIONS:

1. Model one box at a time and have students fill in each box independently. For example, after choosing a topic, model the visualization box and let the children try their visualization skills.

2. As they become more comfortable, introduce subsequent boxes, such as *Who?, What?, Where?, When?, Why?, Feelings,* and *Tell More.* Your pace will vary with your students' abilities.

Tips

✳ Put a blank copy in each student's writing folder for children to use whenever they begin a writing project. The more comfortable and proficient students become with writing skills, the easier it will be for them to get started and the more independent they will become as writers.

✳ Note the relationship between writing and reading as students can use this page to write a literature retelling or a response.

Name: _____ Date: _____

Let's Get Started

 Visualize

 **Who?**

 Why?

 What?

 **Feelings**

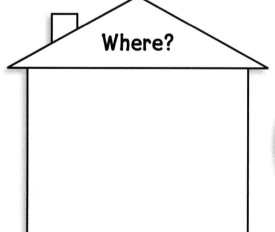 **Where?**

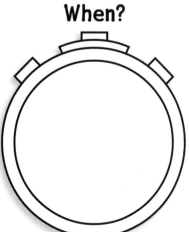 **When?**

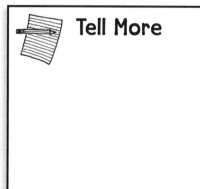 **Tell More**

A Picture Is Worth a Thousand Words

Children will brainstorm a topic by drawing pictures. Drawing pictures can be used as a stepping-stone to brainstorming with words.

BACKGROUND INFORMATION:

Reluctant writers and visual learners often have an easier time starting off using pictures. On a chart pad or dry erase board, model brainstorming with pictures. Keep the pictures simple and remind students that the goal is to spark ideas, not to create a masterpiece. As an extension, use the pictures to create a word list, modeling how the pictures help link related words.

DIRECTIONS:

1 Ask children to write their topic on the easel at the top left of the reproducible.

2 On the two blank sheets of chart paper, have students draw ideas related to their topic. Remind them to keep it simple!

3 Use the lined chart paper to write down related words.

Name: Esperanza   Date: 9-18

A Picture Is Worth a Thousand Words

Topic: baseball team

ball, bat friends, team, coach, practice, assistant coach, batting, first base, ice cream, games, fun

Tips

* Copy this organizer and have it handy during student conferences. When a child has difficulty generating a topic, assist him or her by either drawing on the easel or listing some general ideas on the chart paper.

* The easel can also be used as a place for children to paste photos or magazine pictures to help them spark new ideas and connections for writing.

Name: _____ Date: _____

A Picture Is Worth a Thousand Words

Topic:

Stick Together

Children will organize their ideas by grouping/categorizing similar topics together.

BACKGROUND INFORMATION:

Oftentimes as children begin writing, they struggle with organization. Ideas are mentioned here and there without focus. It is easy for children to drift off topic and to include irrelevant information in their stories. A story about school will often remind a young child about grandma's visit last month. By learning how to group like ideas together, children will be better able to make a point or describe a thought. The lesson here is to stay focused by keeping like ideas together.

DIRECTIONS:

1. On the tape roll, have children write their main topic.

2. On each of the two lists below the tape roll, have children identify two specific details about the main topic. For example, under the main topic *Ocean*, the specific details might be *Animals* and *Things to Do*.

3. Children can draw or write words related to each detail.

Tip

✳ Copy this organizer and encourage students to use it when they need help focusing as they work on independent writing activities.

MORE OPTIONS

✏ Provide children with a main topic and brainstorm details together. Then encourage children to think of ideas related to each detail.

✏ Provide the details and ask children to come up with a main topic.

Name: _____ Date: _____

Stick Together

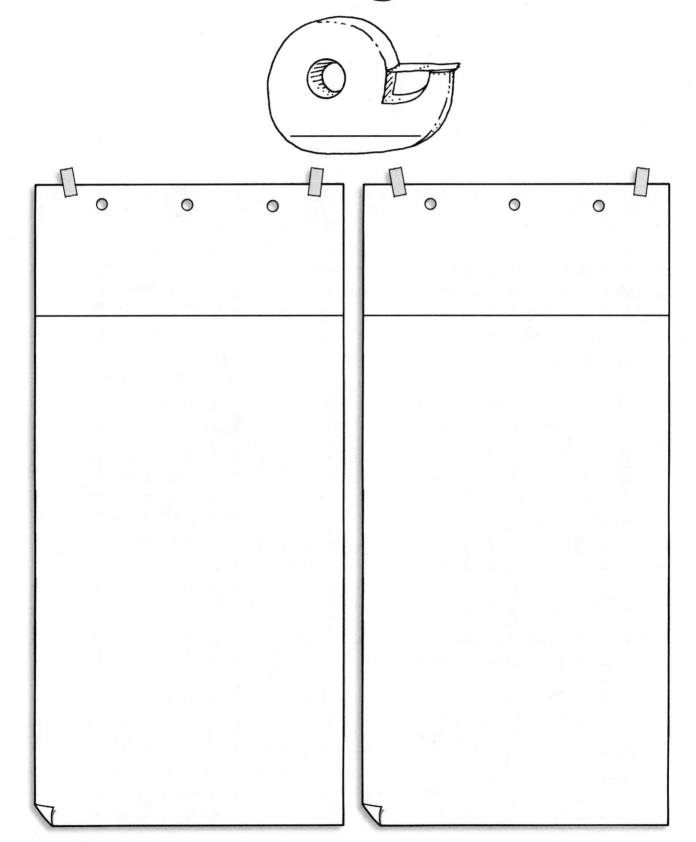

Brainstorm Clusters

Working alone or with a partner, children brainstorm topics, cluster information, and learn how to make associations.

BACKGROUND INFORMATION:

When children are given time to think freely and brainstorm, they become more willing to share ideas and thoughts without always wondering if they are right or wrong. This reproducible can be used as part of the pre-writing phase of the writing process, or as an independent activity to get ideas flowing. Not every idea needs to go through every stage of the writing process. Children can use the brainstorm clusters just to help with idea generation.

DIRECTIONS:

1. Invite children to write or draw their main topic in the center cloud.

2. Have them choose a related detail and write or draw it in the center box at the top of the page.

3. Using that detail as a springboard, children brainstorm related thoughts and put them in the smaller attached boxes.

4. Then, using the main idea in the center cloud again, have children think of another related detail and write that in the center circle at the bottom of the page.

5. Now, using that detail as a springboard, have children brainstorm related thoughts and put them in the smaller attached circles.

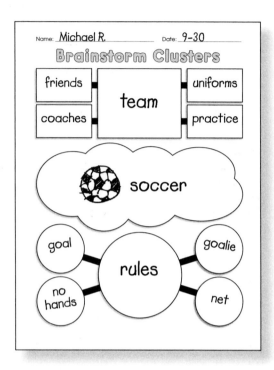

Tip

✳ The shapes help children keep like ideas together.

Brainstorm Clusters

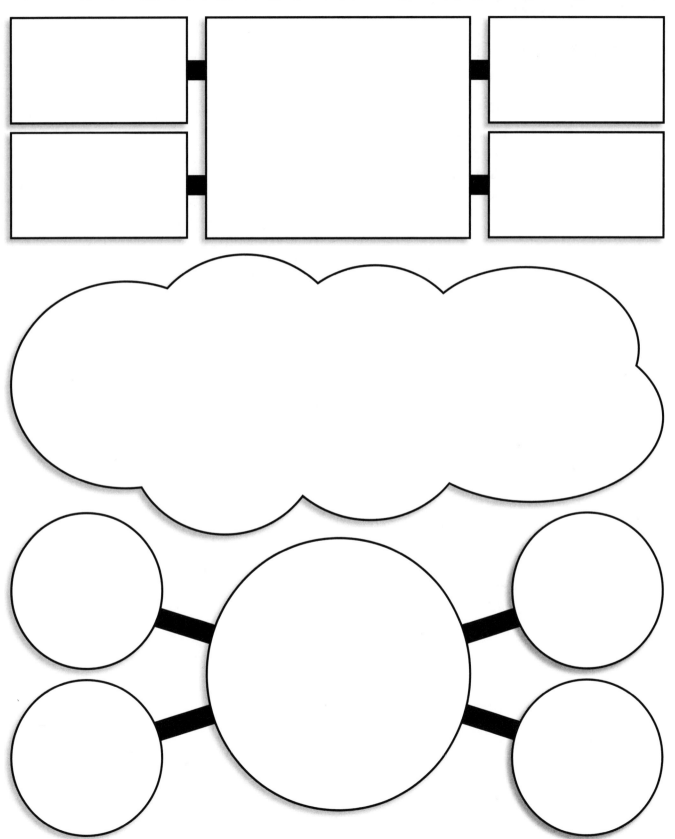

List It!

Children will create lists to help them begin writing about a topic.

BACKGROUND INFORMATION:

Children will be familiar with lists as they have probably experienced shopping lists, wish lists, and birthday lists. Lists can offer children a quick way to generate ideas as well as a way to focus on a topic.

DIRECTIONS:

1 To help generate ideas before writing, have children write or draw their topics in the shopping carts.

2 For each topic, have them create a related list below each cart. This pre-writing activity helps the writer choose a topic and prepare ideas for a rough draft.

MORE OPTIONS

☞ This reproducible can help children feel more comfortable with random brainstorming as well as choosing a topic.

☞ Feel free to supply topics in the beginning, if needed. Children will become more independent as their confidence builds.

☞ Students can use the lists to brainstorm details relating to a specific topic while they are revising.

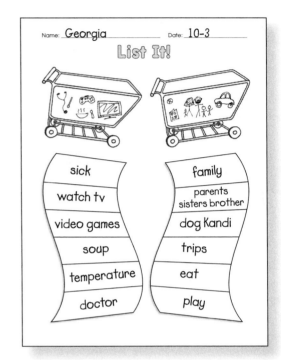

Name: Georgia   Date: 10-3

List It!

sick	family
watch tv	parents sisters brother
video games	dog Kandi
soup	trips
temperature	eat
doctor	play

Tip

✴ Children can illustrate in the carts or, if needed, on the lines.

Name: _____ Date: _____

List It!

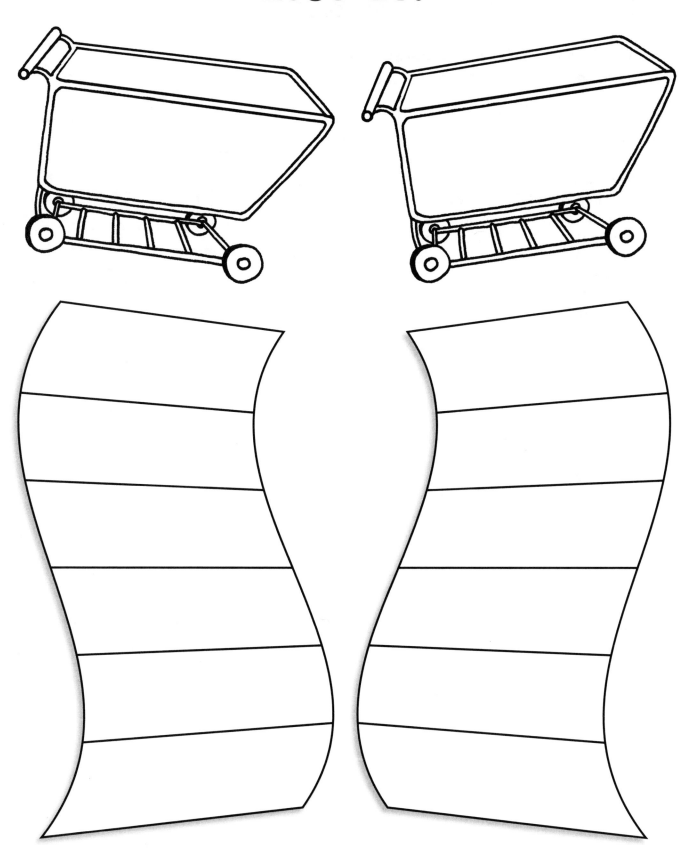

Fragment Fix-It!

Children will differentiate between a fragment and a complete sentence.

BACKGROUND INFORMATION:

Although children will see fragments in stories they read, they need to understand, as beginning writers, how to write complete sentences. Young children should be introduced to sentence basics—a sentence expresses a complete thought, and it contains a subject (who or what) and a predicate (tells about the subject, contains a verb).

DIRECTIONS:

1 Children can work independently, in pairs, or in small groups. Write a sentence fragment in the top pencil.

2 Ask children to change the fragment into a complete sentence and write it in the second pencil.

3 Then write fragments on a chart pad and have children work independently or in pairs to turn the fragments into complete sentences. Children should write their new sentences in the two large pencils at the bottom of the reproducible.

4 Be sure to let students share their sentences aloud.

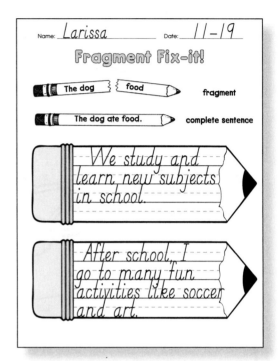

Tip

✳ Keep a stack of this reproducible nearby when conferencing with your students. When a child uses a fragment, write it on a copy of this reproducible to help him or her understand the difference between a fragment and a complete sentence. Put this page in the student's writing folder as a reference.

Name: _____   Date: _____

Fragment Fix-it!

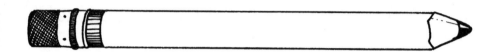 fragment

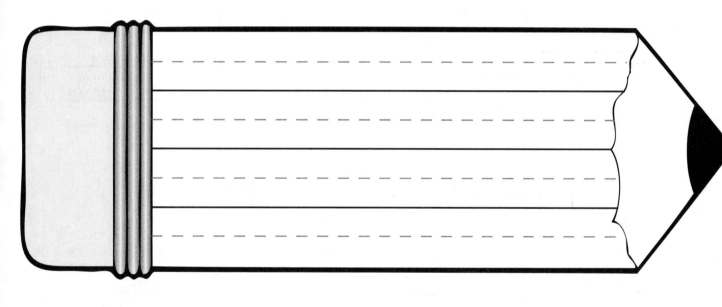 complete sentence

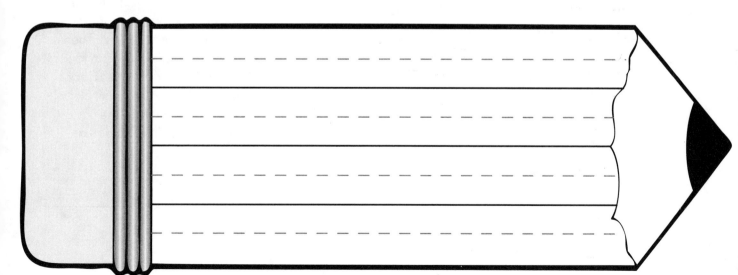

Sentence Strength

Children will learn to write interesting sentences using details.

BACKGROUND INFORMATION:

Young writers often tell the basic facts; for example, *Brian is my best friend*. By teaching children how to include interesting information, they learn to enhance their sentences and improve their overall writing. Tell them that authors often rewrite the same sentence over and over, constantly trying to improve upon it.

DIRECTIONS:

1 Use this reproducible as an independent sentence writing activity. Give children a different topic to write on each weight on the reproducible.

2 Have them practice writing interesting sentences about each given topic.

3 Finally, invite children to read aloud and discuss their sentences.

MORE OPTIONS

✏ Provide a basic topic and have students write a sentence under the first weight. After sharing, discuss ways to improve the sentence by adding appropriate details or interesting language. Then, have children try again under the next weight. Share and note the improvements made.

Name: *Miguel*   Date: *11–26*
Sentence Strength

Brian
topic

Brian is my best friend because we always have fun together.

vacation
topic

During my summer vacation, I will travel to Africa with my family.

Tip

✴ Copy this organizer and have it handy during student conferences. When a child writes a "boring" sentence, give him or her the reproducible and together write an improved sentence under the first weight. Then encourage the student to try writing another sentence under the second weight. Place this page in the student's writing folder as a reference.

Sentence Strength

topic

_____

- - - - - - - - - - - - - - - - - -

_____

- - - - - - - - - - - - - - - - - -

_____

- - - - - - - - - - - - - - - - - -

_____

topic

_____

- - - - - - - - - - - - - - - - - -

_____

- - - - - - - - - - - - - - - - - -

_____

- - - - - - - - - - - - - - - - - -

_____

Bright Ideas

Students will practice writing sentences without having to focus on writing a complete paragraph.

BACKGROUND INFORMATION:

Beginner writers need continuous practice with the basics. Although structured formats may hinder some writers, basic sentence practice is a helpful way to get beginners off to the right start.

DIRECTIONS:

1 In the light bulbs, provide students with topics.

2 Have children write sentences about each topic on the blank lines.

3 Then, invite them to share, discuss, and edit their sentences.

MORE OPTIONS ·····························

✏ Have students use the second light bulb to revise/improve on their first sentence.

✏ Ask children to come up with their own light bulb ideas. Then they can write about their own topics or provide a topic for a friend.

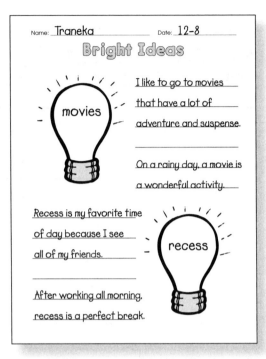

Name: Traneka   Date: 12-8

Bright Ideas

movies — I like to go to movies that have a lot of adventure and suspense.

On a rainy day, a movie is a wonderful activity.

Recess is my favorite time of day because I see all of my friends.

recess

After working all morning, recess is a perfect break.

Tips

✳ Copy this reproducible and have it handy during student conferences. If students need to improve their sentences, they can use the light bulb to refocus and then write an improved sentence on the lines.

✳ Copy this handout and have students use it to write alternative sentences while revising independently or with a peer.

Name: _____ Date: _____

Bright Ideas

_____

_____

_____

_____

_____

_____

_____

_____

Questions

Students will use question words to ask questions about a topic.

BACKGROUND INFORMATION:

A great way to teach children how to elaborate and add more details to their writing is by teaching them how to ask questions. Model this reproducible verbally in small groups or as a whole class. Decide on a topic and ask questions about it. Children will see how much information can be attained. This is a good opportunity to model how all this information can be used in a paragraph.

DIRECTIONS:

1 Write a topic on the clip of the clipboard.

2 Encourage children to use question words to help them formulate questions about the topic.

3 Write the questions on the paper on the clipboard.

4 Then encourage students to use this reproducible as they begin or continue to write about their topics. Remind them to look back at it when they need to add more details.

Tip

✷ Encourage children to get in the habit of asking questions whenever they write. Have blank copies of this reproducible available to students. It will help them add more variety to all of their writing.

Name: _____ Date: _____

Questions

Who? What? Where? Why? Can? Do? Could? How?

Would? When? Will? Should?

Run-On Worms

Students will be able to recognize a run-on sentence and fix it.

BACKGROUND INFORMATION:

Young children are full of information. Hopefully, when they write, they can clearly convey their thoughts. However, most times, they are not thinking about sentences or sentence structure, but only content. This is fine for beginning writers. The important goal, at first, is to get children to share ideas and to express their stories, and not necessarily to focus on their grammar or the structure of their sentences. But, once they are comfortable sharing and they can put their ideas on paper, children do need to be taught how to write a sentence. Without taking away any of their wonderful ideas, we can show children how to eliminate some of the "ands" in their run-on sentences and write more well-constructed, meaningful sentences.

DIRECTIONS:

1 Provide children with the reproducible and give them an example of a run-on sentence.

2 Then show children how to revise the sentence.

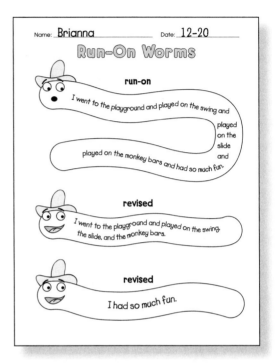

Tip

✳ Copy this organizer and have it handy during student conferences. When a child writes a run-on sentence, give him or her the reproducible and work with the child to write two separate sentences. Place this page in the student's writing folder for reference.

Run-On Worms

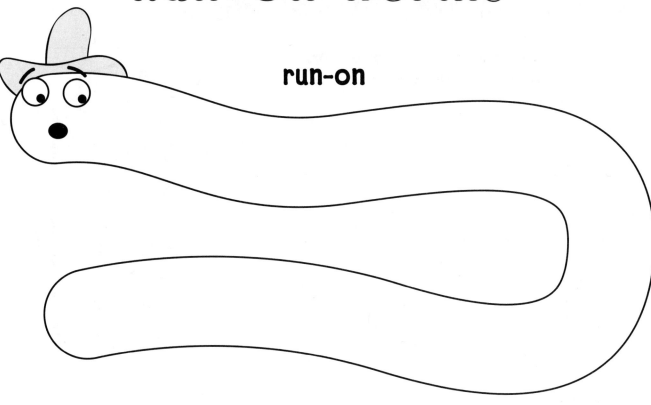

run-on

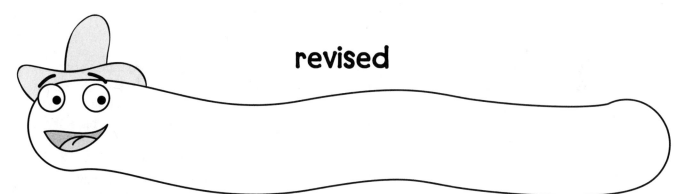

revised

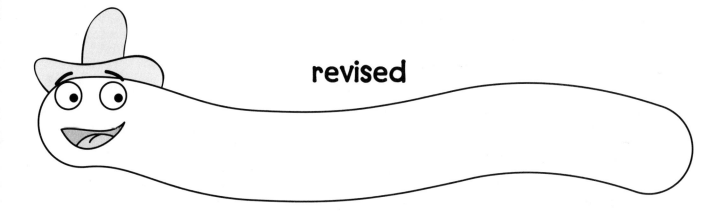

revised

Combining Sentences

Children will learn how to combine short, repetitive sentences into a more meaningful sentence.

BACKGROUND INFORMATION:

Sometimes children write one very long sentence. Sometimes they write lots of short sentences. If beginner writers are actually writing, let them. Celebrate what they do and encourage them to continue expressing themselves. However, when they are clearly comfortable writing, move them forward. Children who are just learning about sentences tend to put periods everywhere. Their stories sound like lists. By teaching children about small connector words, conjunctions (*after, and, but, if, in order that, or, so, than, that, though, until, when, where, while, yet*), children can make their sentences more interesting and more sophisticated.

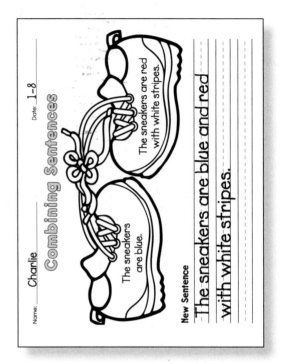

DIRECTIONS:

1 For modeling, present the reproducible with two short, repetitive sentences.

2 Point out that the sentences can be combined to make them better.

3 Show children the parts of the sentences that repeat.

4 Encourage children to combine the sentences to make an improved sentence.

MORE OPTIONS ··

✏ Use examples from students' writing to create the reproducible. Have children edit the sentences and write a sentence combining the information.

Tip

✷ Copy this organizer and have it handy during student conferences. When a student writes multiple short sentences that can be combined, provide the reproducible and edit accordingly. Put this page as a reference in the student's writing folder.

Name: _____

Date: _____

Combining Sentences

New Sentence

_____

_____

_____

_____

First Graphic Organizers: Writing ✳ Scholastic Teaching Resources

Tell More

Children will expand sentences by providing more details.

BACKGROUND INFORMATION:

Children need to be encouraged and taught how to add more details to their stories. It is truly a task to have a child reread his or her work and edit it. By focusing on one sentence at a time, and asking questions, children can expand their sentences to include interesting information.

DIRECTIONS:

1. Provide students with a sentence that lacks detail.

2. Use the boxes below the sentence to add information such as, *Where?*, *When?*, *Why?*, and *How?* as it relates to the original sentence.

3. Model for students how to use the question words to improve the sentence. Provide them with several examples.

4. Then have students work independently to improve their original sentence and rewrite it on the lines below the boxes.

5. Encourage students to reread the sentence to be sure it makes sense.

MORE OPTIONS

✎ Provide examples from students' work for practice. Students can answer the questions by filling in the boxes and then they can rewrite the sentence.

✎ This reproducible can be used in conjunction with a book by writing a basic sentence from the story and having children add more facts (*Where?*, *When?*, *Why?*, and *How?*) to the original sentence.

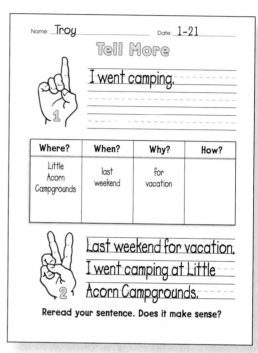

Name: Troy   Date: 1-21

Tell More

I went camping.

Where?	When?	Why?	How?
Little Acorn Campgrounds	last weekend	for vacation	

Last weekend for vacation. I went camping at Little Acorn Campgrounds.

Reread your sentence. Does it make sense?

Tip

✳ Copy this organizer and have it handy during student conferences. When a student writes a sentence lacking detail, give it to him or her to edit the sentence. Place this page in the student's writing folder for reference.

Tell More

1

_____
- -
_____
- -
_____
- -
_____

Where?	When?	Why?	How?

2

_____
- -
_____
- -
_____
- -
_____

Reread your sentence. Does it make sense?

Cut It Out

Children will become more aware of common words and alternative word choices.

BACKGROUND INFORMATION:

Understanding that there are alternative word choices for common words is an important skill for young children. Some words are more popular than others. Some words are too popular! This reproducible encourages children to use a variety of words to express some common feelings and thoughts.

DIRECTIONS:

1 In each of the three boxes across the top of the reproducible, write an overused word, such as *love* or *like*.

2 Help children come up with alternative words for each overused word and write them down on the lines below each box.

MORE OPTIONS

✏ Make posters that show the overused word and its alternatives. Keep adding to this list as the year progresses.

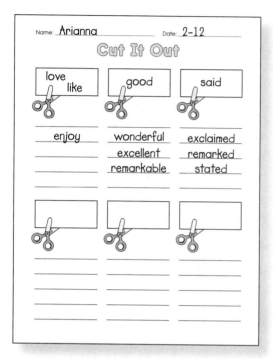

Tips

✳ As shown on the reproducible, if the overused words are similar, they can go in the same box.

✳ Copy this organizer and have it handy during student conferences. When a student uses a common or overused word, have him or her brainstorm alternative word choices and list them on the organizer. Place this page in the student's writing folder for reference.

Name: _____   Date: _____

Cut It Out

Quote Me

Students will learn two ways to write dialogue.

BACKGROUND INFORMATION:

Dialogue makes stories come alive. Dialogue makes stories more interesting. Show children examples of dialogue in literature, comics, and newspapers. Although dialogue can be challenging to write, young children can begin to experiment with different forms of dialogue.

DIRECTIONS:

1 Model the two ways children can write dialogue—using quotation marks or dialogue bubbles. This reproducible gives children the chance to practice both ways.

2 Remind students to add end quotation marks whenever they use beginning quotation marks.

3 Encourage children to decorate the figures below the dialogue bubble.

MORE OPTIONS

✏ Children can work with a partner and create dialogue.

✏ Children can role-play a situation and write a segment of the dialogue.

✏ Children can create an illustration and write related dialogue.

✏ You can present dialogue and have the children write it.

Name: _Gina_   Date: _2-25_

Quote Me

❝ Come to my house to see my new puppy. She is energetic and enjoys playing catch." exclaimed Lee.

Come to my house to see my new puppy. She is energetic and enjoys playing catch!

Tips

✳ This is a good reproducible to keep accessible in the classroom or to put in students' writing folders as a reminder of how to use dialogue when children are just beginning to do so in their writing. The simplicity of this reproducible gives students a chance to think about the conversation they are creating.

✳ Use this reproducible during conferences. Since dialogue is often a new concept to young writers, it will give you a chance to provide some guidance about the use and importance of dialogue.

Quote Me

_____

_____

_____

_____

_____

Indents and Margins

Children will learn how to use margins and how to indent a paragraph.

BACKGROUND INFORMATION:

Young children's early writing experiences are often on drawing paper or unlined paper. The random strings of letters have no form and many times their illustrations speak volumes. That is what we expect from young writers and that is fine. However, when children are introduced to lined paper they often do not understand how to navigate it. They need to learn what the margin is and how to use it. They need to be shown how to indent and how to fill out a line before moving to the next one.

DIRECTIONS:

1. On chart paper, enlarge a sheet of lined writing paper with a margin on it. Use it as a model for this reproducible.

2. Point to the margin and explain its purpose. You might say, "The margin helps you line up your writing."

3. Then show children how to indent. You might say, "When you indent, you start a line of writing a few spaces in from the margin. Every time you write a new paragraph, you indent." If children ask why the first story has both an indentation and skipped lines, but the second only has an indentation, explain that students are leaving room for edits.

4. Now, write a paragraph together and have children copy it to practice indenting and lining up their words with the margin.

5. Point out to students that the right-hand margin warns them that the page is ending.

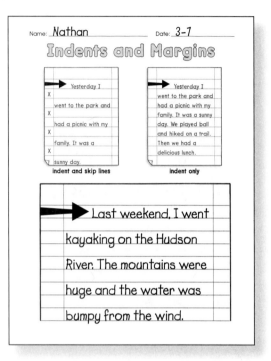

Tip

* This is a good reproducible for children to keep in their writing folders as a reminder to them when they are just beginning to use lined paper for sentence work and paragraph writing.

40

Indents and Margins

→ Yesterday I	→ Yesterday I
X	went to the park and
went to the park and	had a picnic with my
X	family. It was a sunny
had a picnic with my	day. We played ball
X	and hiked on a trail.
family. It was a	Then we had a
X	delicious lunch.
sunny day.	

indent and skip lines   **indent only**

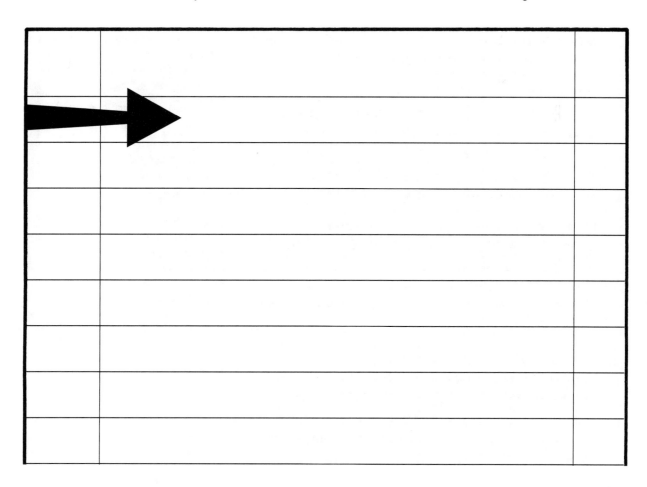

Detailing

Using a topic sentence, children will write related details. Using pertinent details, children will write a topic sentence.

BACKGROUND INFORMATION:

Children will learn about topic sentences and related details and how important they are when writing a paragraph. Children need to know that the topic sentence is the one that tells what the paragraph is about. The related details support, explain, or act as examples to support the main idea. Be sure to model both ways to use this reproducible so children can use it to plan their own writing.

DIRECTIONS:

1. It is imperative to model how to use this reproducible. You can either supply a topic sentence or some details. NOTE: The details can be written or illustrated or both.

2. This versatile reproducible has been designed for students to complete in any order that is most helpful to them. For example, students can start with the topic sentence or the details. Wherever students begin, they then fill in the subsequent information to complete their paragraph plan.

3. To model this lesson, pass out the same reproducible to all students. Then fill in the topic sentence and ask students to supply the details. The next time, supply the details and have students create the topic sentence together. Then have students fill in the information

4. Model often until children understand the benefits of this organizer and how they can use it independently. Writing topic sentences and related details are very difficult skills for young children to master. The more practice they have using them, the easier it will become for students to incorporate them into their own writing.

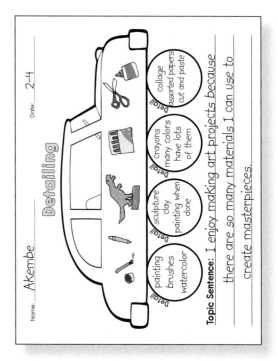

Tips

* This reproducible can also be used during a conference to help a child who may be having difficulty coming up with an appropriate topic sentence or organizing related details.

* Remind students to use this handout to plan their own paragraphs before they begin a rough draft.

42

Name: _____

Date: _____

Detailing

Detail

Detail

Detail

Detail

Topic Sentence: _____
_____

Flowering Paragraph

Children will use this reproducible to organize their ideas for a paragraph.

BACKGROUND INFORMATION:

Almost all young writers need help organizing their thoughts before they begin to write. They must be taught how to make their writing concise, focused, organized, and effective. Planning allows this to happen. Remember, all the components (topic sentence, details, concluding sentence) should be introduced and practiced before children do this independently.

DIRECTIONS:

1 Use this organizer after children have brainstormed (using the Brainstorm Clusters reproducible on page 19 or just a separate sheet of paper) and before they begin their rough drafts. It is an aid to help them with their independent writing.

2 Have students fill in the topic sentence. NOTE: Some students may have difficulty coming up with the topic sentence first. Encourage them to write details to figure out the topic sentence, or suggest that they use the Detailing organizer on page 43 to get started.

3 Using the flowers, have students fill in related details to their topic sentence. They can get these from their brainstorming page. Have them group like topics together.

4 Model how to write a concluding sentence and have students bring their thoughts together in a closing statement.

5 Remind children that they can make changes in their sentences and add new details whenever they feel it is necessary.

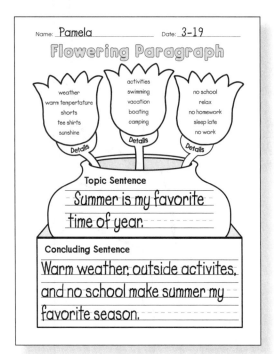

Tip

❋ This reproducible can also be used during a conference to help a child who may be having difficulty coming up with an appropriate topic sentence or organizing related details. Fill in the sections that are working and provide assistance for the parts needing editing.

Name: _____   Date: _____

Flowering Paragraph

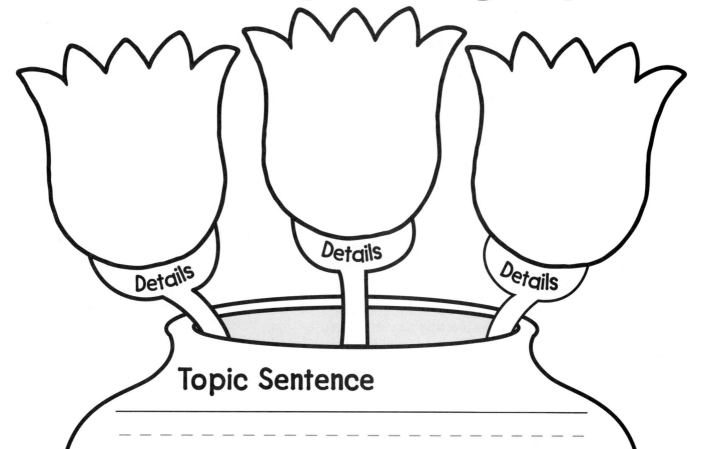

Details

Details

Details

Topic Sentence

Concluding Sentence

Summarize

Children will learn to summarize a story or article and write their summary.

BACKGROUND INFORMATION:

Summaries are a way of using one's own words to focus on the main ideas of a text. It is important for children to understand that they must use their own words to summarize. They also have to understand that when summarizing, they should not include their own thoughts or opinions. A summary stays with the facts, just condensed. By using the 5 W's (*Who?*, *What?*, *Where?*, *When?*, *Why?*), children can identify the key facts and use them to form a concise, accurate summary. Remind children to note the title as well. Be sure to model summarizing as it is a very difficult skill to understand and execute.

DIRECTIONS:

1. Have students identify the 5 W's one at a time. Although the picture clues will assist young learners, summarizing is a more advanced skill and should be taught slowly with plenty of modeling.

2. Once the 5 W's have been identified, help students combine all the key facts into a few sentences. The longer the text is, the longer the summary will probably be, but remind students that summaries should be short.

3. Have students write the summary on the lines below the 5 W's question circles.

Tip

* This reproducible can be used with narrative or expository text and as a literature response.

Name: _____   Date: _____

Summarize

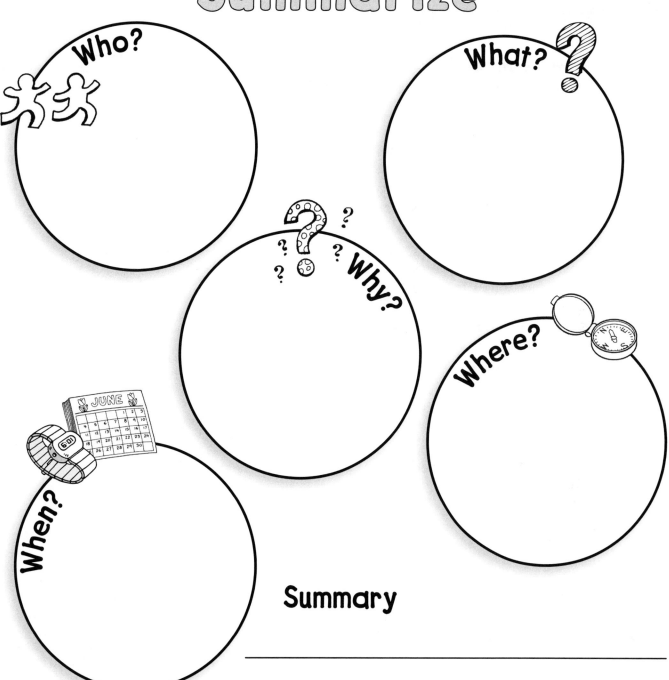

Who?

What?

Why?

Where?

When?

Summary

_____

_____

_____

_____

Narrow the Topic

Children will learn how to focus their ideas and choose a specific topic to write about.

BACKGROUND INFORMATION:

Oftentimes, children will choose a topic that is very general. It is advantageous for children to narrow the topic, allowing them to focus better on specifics and details. By narrowing the topic, the writing task becomes less overwhelming and children can begin to write with greater ease. Model this organizer with the class or a small group. Introduce it as a focused brainstorming activity. Try topics such as those below, encouraging children to narrow the topic.

animals → pets → dogs → Spot

food → restaurants → hamburger restaurants → Bob's Burger Hut

Be aware that children will need a lot of practice narrowing the topic before they can do it independently.

DIRECTIONS:

1 Have children choose a topic to write about. NOTE: Not all topics need to be narrowed.

2 Record the topic on the top line.

3 Encourage students to focus on and narrow their topic.

4 Record the new, narrowed topic on the line under the first topic. (Children may not need to use all the lines to reach a final topic.)

5 When finalized, have children write the topic in the star.

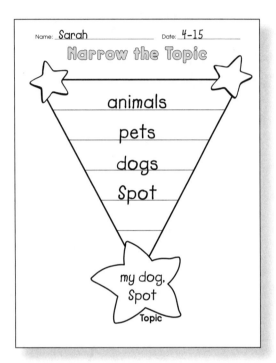

Name: Sarah   Date: 4-15

Narrow the Topic

animals

pets

dogs

Spot

my dog, Spot

Topic

Tips

* This reproducible can also be used during a conference to help a child who may have too broad a topic.

* Remind children that as they begin to write, they may change their topic if the one they started to develop isn't working out as planned.

* Encourage children to use this organizer as needed. Sometimes their topic will be focused right from the start.

Name: _____ Date: _____

Narrow the Topic

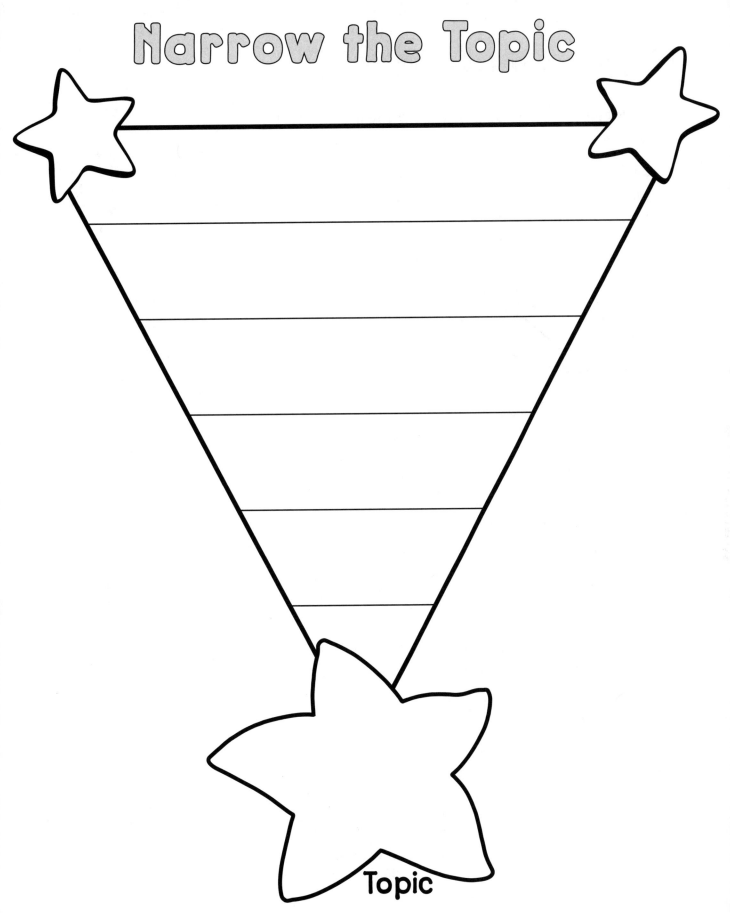

Topic

Revision Ladder

Children will use prompts to help them revise.

BACKGROUND INFORMATION:

When children begin to revise, they may not be sure what to change or fix. This organizer helps students think about specific parts of their work that may benefit from change. With practice and experience, they will begin to think of areas to improve on their own. Model this reproducible using a generic piece of writing or a student's work.

DIRECTIONS:

1. Have students select one area from the reproducible they would like to improve. They can circle it on the reproducible or color code it.

2. Then, using their own work, have them write a sentence from their rough draft, as is, on the top line.

3. Use the blank line next to the chosen ladder rung as a work space for students to rewrite their revised sentence.

4. When the revision is complete, have them transfer their sentence to their rough draft.

5. Then, encourage children to choose another area for revision.

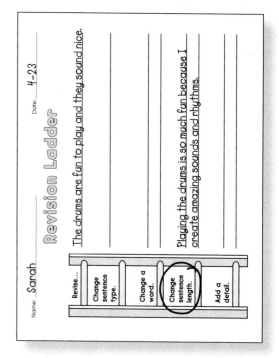

Tip

* This reproducible can also be used during a conference to help a child who may have difficulty revising. Provide suggestions for the parts needing revision.

MORE OPTIONS

✏ An alternative way of using this organizer is to have the student choose a sentence to revise from his or her rough draft and write it, as is, on the top line after "Revise." Then have the student try using *all* the prompts to revise that sentence. This way, students have multiple options to choose from for improving their rough draft.

✏ Have students work with a partner. Children can exchange their writing and make suggestions for each other using the reproducible as a guide. With time, they will think of other suggestions for revisions as well.

Name: _____

Date: _____

Revision Ladder

Revise...				
Change sentence type.				
Change a word.				
Change sentence length.				
Add a detail.				

Fix It Up

Students will choose a section of their own texts to revise.

BACKGROUND INFORMATION:

By encouraging students to reread and look over their work, you will teach them how to make improvements in their writing. Sometimes looking at an entire piece of writing is overwhelming. There is too much to look at, so nothing gets done. Teaching children to look reflectively at small sections at a time allows them to make better changes.

DIRECTIONS:

1 Have students choose a small section of writing from their rough drafts.

2 Instruct them to write it in box 1 at the top of the reproducible.

3 Show students how to underline or highlight parts they would like to change.

4 Then, in box 2, have them make the changes and rewrite the revised sentence.

5 In the saw graphic at the bottom of the reproducible, there is room to remove an off-topic sentence or to rewrite a sentence that may need a word change or a new detail.

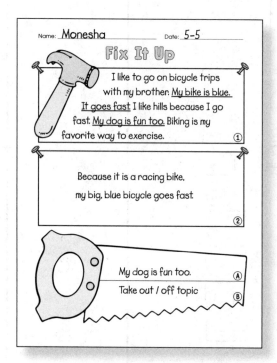

Tip

✳ Use this organizer to model revision techniques by supplying a section of text and allowing children to revise it. If completing this as a class or small group, be sure to encourage children to share, as the discussion can be a valuable lesson.

Fix It Up

1

2

A

B

Stupendous Titles

Using illustrations and key words, students will create possible titles for their stories.

BACKGROUND INFORMATION:

A title is an important part of a story. It can draw someone in and make him or her want to read the story, or it can turn someone off because of its lack of appeal. A title is powerful, so it must be chosen with care.

DIRECTIONS:

1 In the three boxes children can draw or write key words relating to their stories. This will give them focus points.

2 Then on the line below each row of boxes, students should write possible titles. Remind them to choose something that will grab the reader's attention.

3 This is a good time to point out to students the rules of capitalization in titles.

4 Students can use the bottom half of the reproducible to consider other titles.

MORE OPTIONS

✏ As an exercise, give children illustrations or key words and have them come up with titles.

✏ Present children with titles and see if they can tell what the story might be about.

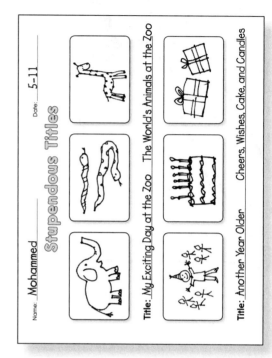

Tip

✳ Share titles of age-appropriate books with children and have them discuss whether or not they like the title of the book and why. This will help children think of titles for their own writing.

Name: _____

Date: _____

Stupendous Titles

Title: _____

Title: _____

Conference Log

This is a reference sheet for you to record students' progress, areas of weakness, and areas of improvement.

BACKGROUND INFORMATION:

Conference time gives you one-on-one time to see the strengths and needs of your students. Although it is generally a short, focused time, it is important to keep track of students' progress. By noting strengths, weaknesses, and areas to work on, you can continue to help children make strides. If the needs of some of your students are similar, you might wish to hold conferences in pairs or small groups. Just remember that keeping records is important to help guide your students as well as to provide accurate information to share with parents. The organizers in this section will assist you in providing mini-lessons or conferences on areas such as spacing and margins, punctuation, sentence structure, adding details, and more.

DIRECTIONS:

1 Make multiple copies of each of the forms at the beginning of the school year and place them in a binder, titled Conference Log.

2 Make a section for each student and put a few log sheets in each child's section.

3 Then, when you begin conferencing, you are all set to record information about each child. The binder will be handy for conferences, report cards, and lesson planning.

Conference Log

Name: Haley

Date	Right-on	Great Improvement	Areas for Improvement
11/28	• word space • capitalization • narrowing topic • getting started	• staying focused • complete sentences	• adding details

Tip

✶ Copy and have these logs available for students before they conference. Give them the opportunity to complete a self-reflection Conference Log on their own. Then use it along with your Conference Log to help students set goals and make progress. Keep all Conference Logs as part of an assessment folder or book.

Conference Log

Date	Right-on	Great Improvement	Areas for Improvement

Word Space

Children will learn to leave space between words when they write.

On this reproducible, "the finger" represents space. (There are pre-made spacers that you can purchase, but the goal is the same.)

Using a Margin

Children will learn to use the left margin to align text properly. They will also learn how to fill a line with text.

Students can use the right margin as a warning that the paper is ending and they should go to the next line.

First Graphic Organizers: Writing ✶ Scholastic Teaching Resources

Lesson: Word Space

The cat is black.

_____

_____

_____

Lesson: Using a Margin

○		

Punctuation: Period

Children will learn what a declarative sentence is and how to punctuate it.

The lines below the sample can be used for students to work on their own sentences. The magic wand at the end of the sentence is a reminder for children to punctuate.

Punctuation: Question Mark

Children will learn what a question is and how to punctuate it.

The lines below the sample can be used for students to work on their own sentences. This reproducible also includes some key question words to help students as they compose. The magic wand at the end is a reminder for children to punctuate.

Punctuation: Exclamation Point

Children will learn what an exclamatory sentence is and how to punctuate it.

The lines below the sample can be used for students to work on their own sentences. The magic wand at the end is a reminder for children to punctuate.

Lesson: Punctuation—Period

- A sentence tells a complete thought.
- A telling sentence makes a statement. It ends with a period.

Baseball is my favorite sport.

_____

_____

_____

_____

_____

_____

_____

_____

Lesson:
Punctuation—Question Mark

- A sentence tells or asks a complete thought.
- An asking sentence asks a question. It ends with a question mark.

Do you like summer vacation ?

_____

_____

_____

_____

_____

_____

_____

Who? What? Where? When? Why? How?
Do? Are? Could? Would? Should? Can?

Lesson:
Punctuation—Exclamation Point

- **A sentence tells a complete thought.**
- **An exclamatory sentence tells something with strong emotion or feeling.**
  It ends with an exclamation point.

The building is on fire!

_____

_____

_____

_____

_____

_____

_____

Indenting

Children will learn how to indent when writing a paragraph.

The example on the left side of the reproducible shows how to indent, and the lines on the right provide space for children to try it independently.

Skipping Lines

Children will learn how to skip lines.

By using little x's (or dots or lines), children will have a visual to remind them which lines to skip. The left side of the reproducible provides an example. The right side provides space for the students to try.

Lesson: Indenting

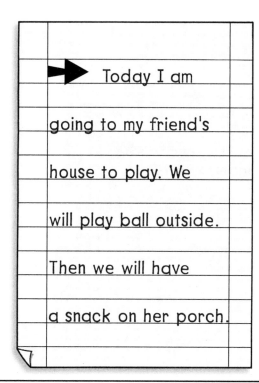

Today I am

going to my friend's

house to play. We

will play ball outside.

Then we will have

a snack on her porch.

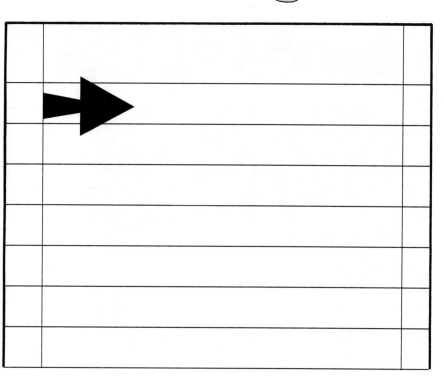

Lesson: Skipping Lines

I just got a

X

new puppy! Her name

X

is Kandi. She is a

X

black standard

X

poodle. Kandi loves

X

to eat treats,

X

especially cheese.

X

Run On and On

Children will learn how to revise a run-on sentence.

The top of the reproducible shows an example of a run-on sentence and how to revise it. The bottom provides space for students to revise their own run-on sentence.

Name: _____ Date: _____

Lesson: Run On and On

It's a beautiful day in the park and the sun is shining and the air is warm because it is finally summer and I'm having fun.

run-on

It's a beautiful day in the park. The sun is shining and the air is warm. It is finally summer and I'm having fun!

revised

run-on

_____

_____

_____

revised

_____

_____

_____

Stay Focused

Children will learn how to remain on topic as they write and revise their work.

Using the bull's-eye drawings, students will decide if the sample sentences are focused and on topic. If the sentence is on topic, it gets a bull's-eye. If the sentence is not on topic, it does not get a bull's-eye. The top portion of the reproducible is an example, and the bottom provides space for a student to use his or her own work.

Name: _____   Date: _____

Lesson: Stay Focused

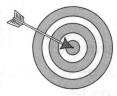 __School is a great place to learn.__

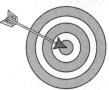 __We study many different subjects.__

 __My dog is cute.__

 __My favorite subject is science.__

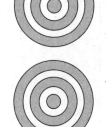 _____

 _____

 _____

_____

Writer's Checklist

The Writer's Checklist is designed to help you and your students keep track of the skills they are acquiring as they become writers. Each child's list will be on his or her level. There are extra writing lines on the reproducible for you to add new skills the child is gaining as his/her experience grows!

Name: _____ Date: _____

Writer's Checklist

- ☐ author's name _____
- ☐ date _____
- ☐ uses proper word space _____
- ☐ uses margins _____
- ☐ uses capital letters correctly _____
- ☐ uses interesting vocabulary _____
- ☐ narrows the topic _____
- ☐ adds details _____
- ☐ stays on topic _____
- ☐ rereads to check for meaning _____
- ☐ uses complete sentences _____
- ☐ checks for fragments _____
- ☐ checks for run-ons _____
- ☐ varies sentence length _____
- ☐ varies sentence type _____
- ☐ uses questions _____
- ☐ uses exclamations _____
- ☐ uses punctuation correctly _____
- ☐ develops a strong topic sentence _____
- ☐ _____

70

Name: _____ Date: _____

Writer's Checklist

☐ __author's name_____

☐ __date_____

☐ _____

☐ _____

☐ _____

☐ _____

☐ _____

☐ _____

☐ _____

☐ _____

☐ _____

☐ _____

☐ _____

☐ _____

☐ _____

☐ _____

☐ _____

☐ _____

☐ _____

About the Author

Rhonda Graff currently teaches second grade at Woodglen Elementary School in New York State. She has been teaching for 18 years, covering first, second, and fifth grades. Rhonda has also taught a Reading Methods course at a local university. This book, *Graphic Organizers for Writing*, is the fifth book she has written for Scholastic Inc. She completed the manuscript for it on the day she finished chemotherapy for breast cancer and feels that both were great accomplishments for her.